3/05 0x 10/03

BAD GUYS

HIGHWAYMEN

BAD GUYS

HIGHWAYMEN

by Gary L. Blackwood

BENCHMARK BOOKS

MARSHALL CAVENDISH
NEW YORK

Benchmark Books
Marshall Cavendish Corporation
99 White Plains Road
Tarrytown, New York 10591-9001
Website: www.marshallcavendish.com

Library of Congress Cataloging-in-Publication Data

Blackwood, Gary L.
Highwaymen / Gary Blackwood.
p. cm. – (Bad guys ; 1)
Includes bibliographical references and index.
Summary: Describes the lives and careers of such European and American highwaymen
as Claude Duval, Mary Frith, and John Thompson Hare.
ISBN 0-7614-1017-1 (library binding)
1. Brigands and robbers—Europe—History—Juvenile literature. 2. Brigands and
robbers—United States—History—Juvenile literature. [1. Robbers and outlaws.] I. Title.

HV6453.E9 B53 2001   364.15′52′094—dc21   99-086663

Book Design by Gysela Pacheco

Photo research by Linda Sykes Picture Research, Hilton Head, SC

Front cover: Private Collection/ Bridgeman Art Library International
Ltd.; pages 2, 19, 54: Hulton Getty/Liaison Agency; pages 7, 9, 11, 14,
17, 18, 24, 35, 44, 46, 48: Mary Evans Picture Library; pages 9, 55: The
Art Archive, London; pages 21, 33: Bettmann/Corbis; page 30: Culver
Pictures; pages 42, 60: Victoria and Albert Musuem/Bridgeman Art Library
International Ltd.; page 51: Bagford Collection/British Museum/ Mary
Evans Picture Library; page 53: Royal Armouries; page 59: William L.
Clements Library, University of Michigan

Printed in Italy

1 3 5 6 4 2

Contents

Introduction

For ordinary folk the figure of the bold and reckless outlaw, the rebel against society, has always held a certain appeal. And no other species of scalawag has been glorified and idealized quite so much as the mounted robbers who haunted the highways of England and America throughout the seventeenth and eighteenth centuries.

They were called—in addition to a lot of less complimentary names—rapparees, High Tobymen, road inspectors, St. Nicholas's clerks, and knights of the road. Today we know them best as highwaymen.

Alfred Noyes's highly romantic and wildly popular 1906 story-poem, "The Highwayman," created almost single-handedly the current popular image of the dashing outlaw on horseback:

> *He'd a French cocked-hat on his forehead, a bunch of lace at his chin,*
> *A coat of the claret velvet, and breeches of brown doeskin:*
> *They fitted with never a wrinkle; his boots were up to the thigh!*
> *And he rode with a jewelled twinkle,*
> *His pistol butts a-twinkle,*
> *His rapier hilt a-twinkle, under the jewelled sky.*

To the common people of their own time, highwaymen seemed just as dashing, even heroic, as Noyes's fictitious hero. As historian Christopher Hibbert points out, the high-wayman "was a rebel, a free man in a society in which those who were not free were exploited and oppressed. A sort of emblematic figure of liberty and pleasure, he was in revolt against the law and against morality. And the imagination of the public has always been more readily caught . . . by the gay and daring sinner than by the humdrum saint."

Most knights of the road did their best to live up to the public's exalted expectations. They considered themselves the upper crust of the underworld, far above the level of the lowly footpad who nicked purses in the crowded streets of London.

The main thing that set the highwayman above and apart from more common criminals was the fact that he owned a horse.

A visitor from France—where brigands were more bru-tal—noted that English highwaymen were, "in general, of a superior class; they pride themselves on having some education and good manners; they even call themselves *gentlemen of the road."*

Many of their number were, in fact, members of the upper classes, especially in the early days of highway robbery. It wasn't at all unusual for the son of a wealthy landowner to spend his entire inheritance on riotous living or wager it away at the gaming tables and then turn thief in order to recover his losses and pay his debts.

Gamaliel Ratsey, one of the earliest English highwaymen, was the son of a Lincolnshire squire. The grotesque mask he donned during holdups, painted with frightening features, earned him the nickname Gamaliel Hobgoblin. Though William Parsons started out with all of the advantages, including a four-thousand-pound endowment from his father, a baronet, he ended up hanging from the gallows like a common thief. James Maclaine, the well-educated son of a Scottish minister, insured his immortality by robbing the noted writer Horace Walpole. Though Maclaine nearly killed him, Walpole admitted that "the whole affair was conducted with the greatest good breeding."

Recorded incidents of highwaymen preying on English travelers date back to the eleventh century. In William Shakespeare's play *Henry IV, Part One*, written around 1597, the unruly Prince Hal and his friend Falstaff find amusement in waylaying "pilgrims going to Canterbury with rich offerings, and traders riding to London with fat purses."

But the real heyday of the highwayman didn't begin until the early seventeenth century. The abrupt boom in roadside robberies can be blamed mainly on three things: 1) the increase in traffic on the main highways, which meant an increase in the number of potential victims; 2) the invention of the flintlock pistol, which was a much more suitable weapon for holdups than a sword or a cumbersome match-lock gun; and 3) the government's refusal to provide any sort of police protection for travelers.

The Statute of Winchester, enacted in 1285, placed the responsibility for controlling crime squarely on the shoulders of the local authorities. Cesar de Saussure, a French visitor to England, explained how this "queer law" worked. If a traveler "is robbed . . . in the daytime and on the high road, and if he declares the theft to the sheriff of the county before the sun sets . . . the county in which he has been robbed is obliged to refund him the sum."

The system wasn't very effective. For one thing, most thieves operated after dark, not in broad daylight. For another, dishonest travelers took advantage of the law. They would arrange to be robbed temporarily, and then would collect their consolation prize from the county and split the profits with the "robbers."

Ultimately, honest travelers had only two choices in dealing with thieves: carry pistols and try to defend themselves, or give up their gold when they heard the highwayman's familiar command, "Stand and deliver!"

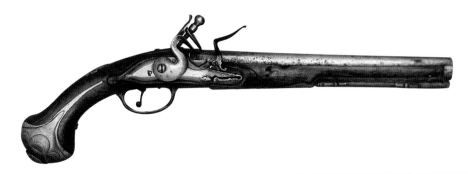

The flintlock pistol. "The true father of Highwaymen," writes crime historian Patrick Pringle, "was the inventor of firearms."

One

The Roaring Girl

For the most part highway robbery was men's work. As essayist Thomas De Quincey noted, a good highwayman must have "strength, health, agility, excellent horsemanship, intrepidity of the first order, presence of mind, courtesy. . . . The finest men in England, physically speaking . . . were the mounted robbers."

But one of the earliest and most notorious English highwaymen was a woman. What's more, she took up the trade at a rather advanced age. Mary Frith, a London shoemaker's daughter, was born around 1584. According to a chapbook of the time, Mary was a "lusty and sturdy child" with "a voice that will drown all the city."

Early on she began showing signs that she was not likely to adhere to the accepted standards of femaleness. "A very tomrig or rumpscuttle she was, and delighted and sported only in boys' play and practice, not minding or companying with the girls." She became so unmanageable that her parents actually attempted to ship her off to America as an indentured servant; Mary slipped away before the ship sailed.

To support herself she turned thief, working the crowds that gathered in the vicinity of St. Paul's Cathedral. While an accomplice created a diversion, Mary

Though she dealt in stolen goods, Moll Cutpurse was considered scrupulously honest and generous by her colleagues. Thieves who were down on their luck could always count on her for help.

deftly cut her chosen victim's purse strings. Her skill earned her the nickname Moll Cutpurse. But Mary wasn't content to be a common cutpurse. Dissatisfied with the paltry prices she got selling her take to the local fences, or receivers of stolen goods, she went into business as a fence herself, and gained such a reputation for fair dealing that she soon drove the other receivers out of business.

By the time she was in her late twenties, Moll Cutpurse had become such a well-known figure that noted playwrights Thomas Middleton and Thomas Dekker staged a very successful comedy about her, titled *The Roaring Girle*—a reference to Mary's oversized voice. She also turned up as a character in Nathaniel Field's play *Amends for Ladies* and in a book called *The Madde Prancks of Merry Moll of the Bankside.*

Mary grew so wealthy from reselling ill-gotten goods—often to their original owners—that she bought a large house and employed three maids and a footman. But apparently she went on stealing on the side. She was arrested at least four times and each time the letter *T* was branded on one of her hands—the punishment for petty theft.

When London authorities forced her to make a public confession of her crimes, she broke down and "wept bitterly, and seemed very penitent"—probably less from any real remorse than from the fact that "she was maudlin drunk, being discovered to have tippeled of three quarts of sack [wine]."

When she was in her sixties, Mary suddenly

branched out in a new direction. She became a lady of the road. Perhaps she found life as a fence and an occasional footpad unfulfilling. Or it may be that she needed the money, for her earnings dropped off sharply when England turned from a monarchy to a republic.

The king, Charles I, was defeated and dethroned by an army of dissidents known as Parliamentarians, or Roundheads, who wanted the growing middle class to have more say in the government. After Charles I was executed in 1649, England, together with Ireland and Scotland, became the Republican Commonwealth and Protectorate. Oliver Cromwell, the military leader of the Roundheads, was named its Lord Protector.

Many of those who had supported the king lost their fortunes and estates, and were forced into the only occupation suitable for a gentleman—highway robbery. Most made it a point to waylay only Roundheads. According to legend, the Lord Protector himself was robbed at least twice; once the thief supposedly crowned Cromwell with a chamber pot.

Even highwaymen who weren't from the upper class tended to be staunch Royalists, people who favored letting the nobility keep their estates and their power. After all, if there were no rich ruling class to rob, the pickings would be much leaner.

Moll Cutpurse shared these sentiments. Her most renowned victim was Sir Thomas Fairfax, a general in the Roundhead army. In her typical brazen fashion, Mary single-handedly accosted Fairfax and his two servants on Hounslow Heath, near London, in broad daylight. When the general resisted, she shot him in the arm, then shot the servants' horses out from under them.

Mary was pursued anyway, but might have escaped if her horse had not gone lame. She was captured, tried, and sentenced to be hanged. But the punishment was never carried out. Mary blithely bought herself a pardon for the considerable sum of two thousand pounds, and returned to her old career as a fence.

The Roaring Girl died of dropsy in 1659, at the ripe age—for those days—of seventy-five. Though she missed the Restoration—the return of Charles II to the

Opponents of the English king, such as Sir Thomas Fairfax, were favorite targets of highwaymen.

throne—by a year, she did leave her friends twenty pounds in her will so they could celebrate the event. She also left instructions that she be buried with her rear end pointing upward, so she could remain as outrageous in death as she had been in life.

Two

The French Footman

When Charles II regained the throne, his loyal supporters regained their positions of privilege and power. Many who had turned thief gave up their criminal careers. The outlaws who remained on the roads had less competition and, at the same time, more wealthy targets to choose from.

Though the new breed of highwaymen mostly came from humble backgrounds, they tried hard to maintain their image as chivalrous knights of the road. A German writer of the time observed that they were "generally very polite; they assure you *they are very sorry that poverty has driven them to that shameful recourse,* and end by demanding your purse in the most courteous manner." As long as their demands were promptly met, anyway.

A few remained gallant even in the face of resistance, especially if the victim was of the female persuasion. When a young married woman informed her assailant that she "would sooner part with life" than with the ring on her finger, he replied, "Since you value the ring so much, madam, allow me the honour of saluting the fair hand which wears it, and I shall deem it a full equivalent!" With that he bent, kissed the lady's hand, and rode away—but not without her purse.

More often, uncooperative travelers were subjected to a barrage of threats and insults—and sometimes far worse. Irish outlaw Patrick Fleming cut off the nose, lips, and ears of a man who was foolish enough to refuse him. When a woman was too slow in handing over her diamond ring, highwayman Thomas Wilmot impatiently chopped off her finger. William Cady, a surgeon's renegade son, was even more ruthless; when a victim swallowed her ring rather than give it up, Cady shot her, then slit her open to retrieve it.

Incidents like these, which were far from rare, made it clear that underneath the veneer of chivalry and courtesy, highwaymen were desperate and dangerous criminals. Still, many well-bred Englishwomen insisted on regarding them as romantic figures, especially if, like the celebrated French outlaw Claude Duval (or Du Vall), they had the added attraction of a foreign accent.

Though Duval became legendary for his gallantry and good breeding, he was not born a gentleman; his father was a miller, his mother a tailor's daughter. Claude was born in Normandy in 1643. At fourteen he made his way to Paris, where, according to a biographical pamphlet, he lived "unblameably, unless you esteem it a fault to be scabby, and a little given to filching [stealing]."

By the age of seventeen he had found honest work as a footman for an English nobleman who had exiled himself to France to await the return of his king. When the Restoration came, Claude's employer returned home, taking Claude with him.

Before he gained fame as a dashing highwayman, Claude Duval fleeced folk by pretending he could turn ordinary metal into gold.

Footmen, for some reason, were prime candidates for a criminal career. Duval's success as a thief may well have started the trend. Within a few years of his arrival in England, he was the leader of a small band of brigands—and also led the *London Gazette*'s list of most wanted highwaymen.

He was having equal success with women. According to his biographer, William Pope, women of all sorts—"maids, widows and wives, the rich, the poor, the noble, the vulgar"—found the handsome Frenchman irresis-

Dr. Pope's accounts of Duval's gallantry, meant to be satirical, were taken seriously by later historians, one of whom called the French footman "an eternal feather in the cap of highway gentility."

tible. This "great fondness of English ladies towards French footmen," wrote Pope, " . . . was a too common complaint."

In his *Memoirs of Du Vall*, Pope recounts a possibly fictitious incident that portrays Duval the way the ladies wished to see him. In the story, Duval and his men stop a coach containing a nobleman, his lady, and four hundred pounds in gold. To show her fearlessness, the lady calmly takes out a flute and plays a tune.

Criminal Justice

Any history of highwaymen is liable to give the impression that nearly all of them ended up on the gallows. That's because the robbers we know the most about are the ones who were caught and who had their confessions recorded (and then printed and sold at a halfpenny apiece) by the ordinary, or chaplain, of London's Newgate prison.

There were of course any number of highwaymen who escaped justice entirely. Even those who were caught were not necessarily hanged; a nonviolent thief might only be transported—sent off to the American colonies to work on a plantation. (After America won its independence, Australia became the destination for transported convicts.)

A few robbers retired before it was too late and went on to respectable careers. The most illustrious of these was Sir John Popham, who, after a decade as a "road inspector," was persuaded by his wife to give it up. He studied law, was elected to Parliament, became a member of Queen Elizabeth I's Privy Council, was appointed Attorney General, and finally, in 1592, was knighted and named Lord Chief Justice. His Lordship was, it is said, especially hard on highwaymen.

Prisoners had to pay for the privilege of lodging in the Middle Ward of Newgate prison. Those who couldn't afford it were consigned to the damp, dark cells of the Lower Ward.

When an acquaintance from his criminal past was brought before him, Sir John asked what had become of all their old companions. The man replied, "All the villains are hanged, my lord, except you and me."

"Sir," says Duval, "your lady plays excellently, and I doubt not but that she dances as well." With the permission of the lady's husband, the brigand dances her gracefully about the heath. As the coach is about to depart, Duval reminds the husband that "you have forgot to pay the musick." The man hands over only a third of the money, but Duval accepts it graciously and "civilly takes his leave."

The Frenchman was not always so civil. Another of his victims was a young mother who was feeding her baby from a silver bottle. Duval greedily snatched the bottle out of the baby's mouth. When one his fellow accomplices pointed out how damaging this incident would be to his reputation, Duval grudgingly returned the fancy bottle.

Like most members of his profession, Duval was a little too fond of strong drink, and it led to his downfall. In 1670, as he was in London's Hole in the Wall tavern celebrating a successful holdup, someone recognized him and sent for the local bailiff. Too drunk to resist, Duval was hauled off to Newgate, where he was sentenced to be hanged.

Though he was only twenty-seven, he was so famous that "crowds of ladies visited him in the condemned hold," some so well known that they wore masks to conceal their identity. Several pleaded tearfully with the king to spare Duval's life. But when the judge threatened to resign if Duval was pardoned, the death sentence was carried out.

OLD NEWGATE PRISON.

In 1780 Newgate prison was burned by rioters, and the prisoners—many of whom were highwaymen—were set free, creating a sudden surge in highway robbery.

Duval's admirers gave him a fine funeral and a marble gravestone that read:

> *Here lies Du Vall: Reader, if Male thou art,*
> *Look to thy purse; if Female, to thy heart.*
> *Much havoc has he made of both; for all*
> *Men he made stand, and women he made fall.*

Soon after Duval's execution, Pope, a respected doctor and a professor of astronomy at Oxford, published the *Memoirs of Du Vall.* Though this slim pamphlet was meant to poke fun at the tendency to glamorize highwaymen, it had quite the opposite effect. Most readers, including historians who read it a century or two later, overlooked the book's subtle satire. Instead of deflating Duval's reputation, Pope added to it. *Memoirs* was so popular that it inspired a steady stream of imitators. For the next hundred years hardly a highwayman went to the gallows at Tyburn without some opportunist in the crowd hawking a hastily printed—and usually fanciful—account of the man's life and crimes.

Three
The Yorkshire Rogue

Because the roads near London were the most heavily traveled in England, they saw the most criminal activity. Highwaymen liked to lie in wait on lonely stretches of moorland or beside steep hills, where coaches slowed almost to a halt. The appropriately named Shooter's Hill on the road to Dover was a favorite spot for an ambush.

Gad's Hill near Rochester was well known as thieves' territory even in Shakespeare's time. The robbery in *Henry IV, Part One* takes place there; in fact, one of the robbers is nicknamed Gadshill. Daniel Defoe's 1724 book, *Tour through the Whole Island of Great Britain*, describes the hill as "a noted place for robbing of seamen, after they have received their pay at Chatham."

Highway robbery was by no means confined to the London area though. One of the most fabled highwaymen operated some two hundred miles away, in the rural northern county of Yorkshire (now three separate counties). In spite of being off the beaten path, William Nevison made his name and exploits known throughout England. Shortly after his execution, a London publisher issued a popular chapbook titled *The Yorkshire Rogue*, only one of a wealth of broadsheets and ballads based on Nevison's deeds.

Though he operated mostly in the far north of England, William Nevison's reputation was so widespread that the king issued a proclamation calling for the highwayman's arrest and offered a reward.

There are also plenty of official documents chronicling his career. Yet the facts about his life and crimes are confused and contradictory. Some sources of the time refer to him as *John* Nevison. Records at York Castle indicate that his "real name was John Brace, or Bracy." This was probably a misunderstanding; apparently Nevison sometimes used the name of his accomplice, Edward Bracy, as an alias.

The place and date of his birth are disputed too. All that's certain is that he was born in Yorkshire around 1639. According to one biographical pamphlet, Nevison was wayward even as a boy. A "lusty, well-looking lad," he was "the ringleader of all his young companions in rudeness and debauchery."

At fourteen he stole ten pounds from his father and a horse from the local schoolmaster, and headed for London. So that no one could use the horse to trace him, he slit its throat. For three years he held down an honest job as a brewer's apprentice, but apparently concluded that stealing was easier. With two hundred pounds of his master's money he took off to Holland.

Described as "tall in stature, every way proportionable, exceeding valiant, having also the air and carriage of a gentleman," Nevison was evidently attractive to women; in Holland he met and married the daughter of a rich merchant. The two helped themselves to her father's money—and landed in prison for it. Nevison at once engineered an escape, the first of many, leaving his new wife behind. Legend has it that she died of a broken heart.

Nevison fled to the French province of Flanders, where he served with the English army. Then, finding it not to his liking, he deserted. Back in England, he began his career as a highwayman, first in the London area and then in Yorkshire. He quickly gained a reputation as a sort of Robin Hood, robbing from the rich and giving to the poor. His generosity seems not to have extended to the middle class; he collected quarterly payments from cattle drovers and teamsters that guaranteed he would "let them passe quietly."

At some point he was captured and thrown into Wakefield prison, but readily escaped. It may have been at about this time that Nevison performed the feat of endurance and horsemanship that earned him lasting fame—if indeed he was the one who perfomed it.

As with many other elements of his life, the truth of the matter may never be known. But according to popular tradition, in or about 1676 Nevison returned to his old hunting grounds near London, perhaps because the law in Yorkshire was breathing down his neck. Early one morning he held up a gentleman at Gad's Hill, making no attempt to disguise his identity. Then, according to Daniel Defoe's account, "holding on the North Road, and keeping a full larger gallop most of the way," he rode the two hundred miles back to York, arriving at around 7 P.M. After stabling his horse—surely not the same one he started out on; few mounts could have survived such a grueling trip—he donned fresh clothes and hurried to the town bowling green, where the Lord Mayor of York was playing. Nevison cornered His Lordship and made a point of asking "what o'clock it was."

Though the victim positively identified Nevison as the man who had robbed him at Gad's Hill, the Lord Mayor of York swore that Nevison had been in Yorkshire at eight o'clock that evening. Since "it was impossible the man could be at two places so remote on one and the same day," Nevison went free.

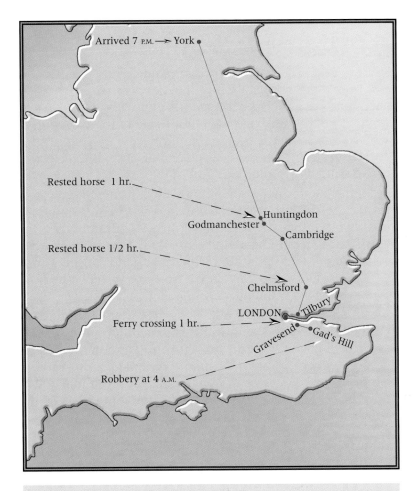

In his book Tour through the Whole Island of Great Britain, *Daniel Defoe recounted the story of Swift Nicks and traced the likely route of the robber's amazing ride.*

Later, the king himself asked Nevison "on assurance of pardon and that he should not be brought into any further trouble about it, to confess the truth." Nevison admitted to the robbery and to making the unheard-of ride. "Upon this the King gave him the name or title of Swift Nicks," because even the devil himself, known

The Highwayman without a Country

Most highwaymen preferred to work in familiar surroundings, within reach of several "safe houses"—inns or residences where they could lie low without fear of being betrayed. But knowing that if they always stayed close to home they were more likely to be caught, some ventured farther afield. It was a common practice for English thieves to travel across the Channel to Europe and dispose of their goods there, so the valuables couldn't be traced.

Occasionally a criminal came along who considered any and all countries part of his territory. Such a man was Joseph Mountain, possibly the only black highwayman on record. Mountain, whose mother was a slave, was born in Philadelphia in 1758. At seventeen he sailed to London, where he fell in with a band of brigands posing as traveling musicians and jugglers; this was only a front to conceal "the principal business of their lives, viz. highway robbery."

As Mountain wrote in his confessions, when one of the gang was captured, he "resolved to quit this course of life" and signed on as cook on a sailing ship. But on his return to London he took up his old profession, which, "though singularly vicious, yet possessed many charms in my view." For several years he ranged from one end of England to the other, robbing all the way. Then, around 1779, he married the wealthy "miss Nancy Allingame, a white girl of about eighteen." After three years, having "exhausted all the property that came into my possession by the marriage," he tried his luck in France, then Holland, then Spain—in fact, Mountain claimed, he "robbed in most of the capital cities of Europe."

It wasn't until he returned to the United States that he was finally apprehended—not for theft, but for assaulting "a respectable young girl" outside of New Haven, Connecticut. "There can be no excuse given for me," he wrote, "unless intoxication [being drunk] may be plead in mitigation."

Mountain expressed confidence that "in a country where such a sacred regard is had to the liberty of the subject, no man's life can be unjustly taken from him." Nevertheless, like so many of his colleagues, Joseph Mountain ended his life and career at the end of a rope.

as Old Nick, could not have ridden the distance any more swiftly.

Defoe fails to mention Swift Nicks's real name. Though Yorkshire legend gives Nevison the credit for the amazing ride, nineteenth-century historian Thomas Babington Macaulay observed that the same feat had been attributed to a number of different highwaymen (including, as you will see in Chapter Six, the famous Dick Turpin).

One thing that Nevison can reliably lay claim to is an uncanny aptitude for getting out of prison. Remember that he had already escaped twice. In 1676, the same year he supposedly made his amazing ride, he was detained in the super-secure York Castle. Nevison didn't exactly escape, but he did find a way out. He was forced to join an army company headed for Tangier, and promptly deserted.

Soon Nevison was arrested again, and jailed in Leicester. This time his jailers shackled his hands and feet and guarded him closely. Seventeenth-century prisons were unhealthy places, and it wasn't long before Nevison fell ill. A doctor examined him and diagnosed that dread disease, the plague. A few days later the doctor carted away Nevison's lifeless body, to the great relief of his jailers and of the wealthy residents thereabouts, who could now travel about safely—or so they thought.

After dark on the very day Nevison was buried, a traveler was held up by what he swore was the dead highwayman's ghost. It was of course Nevison in the flesh. And the "doctor" had been an accomplice who gave Nevison a drug that made him appear to be dead.

In 1681 Nevison was detained in York Castle yet again, and managed to escape yet again. By now there was a price of twenty pounds on his head, and the land-

William Nevison's death on the York gallows was mourned by many—especially tavern owners. As a diarist of the time noted, "He hath left much debt at severall alehouses in the country where he haunted."

lady of the Plough Inn, where the highwayman often laid low between holdups, decided to collect it. She agreed to alert the local authorities the next time Nevison turned up. On March 6, 1684, she dispatched this message: "The Bird is in the cage."

At midnight a constable broke into Nevison's room, bound him, and escorted him to York Castle for the third and final time. After thirty years on the run, Nevison was, according to a popular ballad, resigned to his fate:

> *I've not robb'd the poor of twopence,*
> *I've neither done murder nor kill'd,*
> *But guilty I've been all my lifetime,*
> *So, gentlemen, do as you will.*
> *. . . My peace I have made with my Maker,*
> *And with you I'm quite ready to go;*
> *So here's adieu to this world and its vanities,*
> *For I'm ready to suffer the law.*

The law sentenced him to be hanged, and this time there was no escape.

Four
The Golden Farmer

Most highwaymen didn't escape justice nearly as long as Swift Nicks or Moll Cutpurse did. More typical were the careers of thieves such as Jack Sheppard and the father-son team of John Beatson and William Whalley. Though Sheppard was a celebrated criminal, his fame was due more to his skill in escaping from jail cells than to his abilities as a thief. In fact, his foray into highway robbery lasted only about a week and netted him all of thirty shillings. Beatson and Whalley committed only a single robbery—the 1801 holdup of a Royal Mail coach—before they were caught and hanged.

The fatal flaw common to most highwaymen was a lack of imagination. A disguise seems like an obvious precaution, but few thieves bothered with one. Some did wear a black mask over the eyes, or a handkerchief over the lower face; others merely pulled down the brim of their tricornered hat to conceal their features.

After a holdup, instead of making himself scarce, the typical robber headed for a tavern, where he squandered his spoils on women, drink, and gambling. As Prince Hal observes in *Henry IV, Part One*, a "purse of gold most resolutely snatch'd on Monday night" was generally "most dissolutely spent on Tuesday morning."

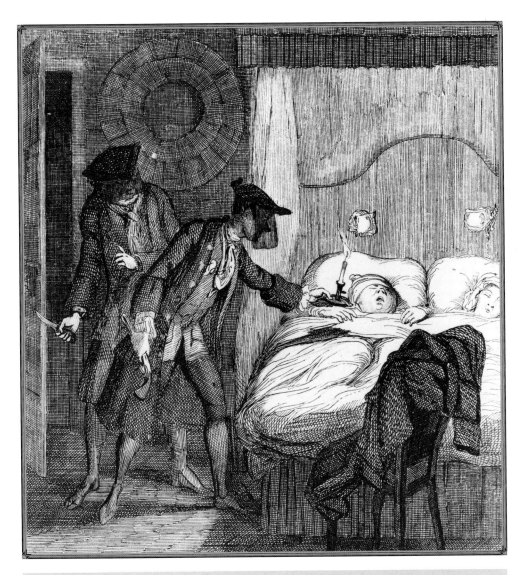

Jack Sheppard, pictured here with an accomplice called Blueskin, was so small and slim that he escaped from one prison cell by squirming up the chimney.

One notable exception was William Davis, who practiced the profession for more than forty years—probably an all-time record. Incredibly, in all that time no one close to him, not even his wife or his eighteen children, was aware of his illegal activities, for Davis led a double life.

Most people knew him as a hardworking, respected family man who leased a prosperous farm in Gloucestershire. But Davis also had a dark and disreputable side. His land bordered Bagshot Heath, one of the most robbery-prone places in England. When the demands of being a pillar of the community weighed too heavily, Davis went riding on the heath—taking with him a mask, a wig, and a brace of loaded pistols.

Though most of St. Nicholas's clerks preferred to work the night shift, Davis was so confident of his disguise that he often held up his victims in broad daylight. He was no Robin Hood. Though he regularly robbed the rich, including the Duchess of Albemarle, he didn't hesitate to relieve a traveling tinker—a mender of pots and pans—of his last shilling. According to a contemporary account, when the tinker protested that he was a hundred miles from home and would be reduced to begging, Davis replied, "I don't care if you have to beg your way two hundred miles, for if a tinker escapes Tyburn and Banbury [gallows], it is his fate to die a beggar."

Somehow, Davis even managed to rob local merchants without their ever suspecting his identity. The fact that he paid all his debts in gold coin should have raised some eyebrows, but apparently it only made his neighbors admire him more; they even nicknamed him the Golden Farmer.

A familiar tavern was one of the few places where a robber on the run felt safe. Ironically, many highwaymen were captured in such establishments while their guard was down.

His most audacious stunt was robbing his own landlord, who had just collected the annual rent of seventy guineas. As soon as the man left, Davis donned his usual disguise and, taking a shortcut, ambushed him.

The landlord cried, "What, have you no pity, religion, or compassion in you? Have you no conscience?"

"I have no more of that dull commodity than you have," replied the robber, "nor do I allow my soul and body to be governed by religion, but by interest."

Eventually Davis pursued his interests farther and farther from home, where he was not so likely to be recognized. In 1690, when he was sixty-three, the Golden Farmer stopped a coach on the Exeter highway —a routine robbery for such a seasoned highwayman. But Davis's confidence must have made him careless; he neglected to search the passengers for firearms.

As he rode away, a man in the coach produced a pistol and fired. Wounded, the highwayman toppled from his horse and was captured. When Davis revealed his long history of deception and duplicity, it caused a sensation throughout the country.

Though highwayman Francis Jackson once claimed that "he can't be hanged . . . who hath Five Hundred Pounds at his Command," all of Davis's stolen gold failed to save him. After his execution, his body hung in chains from a gibbet on Bagshot Heath as a warning to young men who were tempted to follow in the Golden Farmer's footsteps.

Five

The Derry Outlaw

As the seventeenth century came to a close, so did the glory days of the English highwayman. In league with several other countries, England had been at war with France for most of a decade. When the hostilities—known as the War of the Grand Alliance—ended in 1697, hundreds of unemployed British soldiers found a new use for their fighting skills: highway robbery. This influx of ill-mannered, ill-educated military men severely tarnished the once shining image of the gentleman thief. But across the Irish Sea, the tradition of the robber as a romantic Robin Hood still flourished.

After resisting English domination for centuries, embattled Irish chieftains had at last given up their vast estates and fled Ireland. Settlers from England and Scotland promptly took control of the land, leasing sections of it to Irish farmers. Rents were often outrageous, and those who couldn't pay were evicted.

Predictably, many dispossessed farmers "went on their keeping"—turned outlaw, in other words. The most celebrated of these rapparees, as they were called, was Shane Crossagh of County Derry.

The Derry Outlaw was born John O'Mullan, around 1670. ("Shane" is a variation of "John"; "Crossagh," meaning "pockmarked," was a title the family used to distinguish themselves from other O'Mullans.) Shane and his parents had been driven from their tenant farm and were leading a meager, hand-to-mouth existence in the mountains.

Hoping that his family might someday return to the farm, Shane made secret forays to keep the place from falling into disrepair. Two soldiers spotted him and charged him with trespassing. Though Shane was a tall, powerfully built lad with a reputation as a fighter, he surrendered meekly, only asking permission to retrieve a hidden jug of poteen, or homemade whiskey, from the bushes. What he'd actually concealed there was a pike, a spearlike weapon, which he then used to rout the soldiers.

This defiance of authority made Shane a wanted man. Though his family advised him to give himself up, Shane refused. He and two friends hid out in the hills in a sod hut and set about robbing the greedy landowners. Less wealthy folk were safe as long as they paid a quarterly "tax" of ten pence to the thieves. The genuinely poor had nothing to fear; in fact, Shane gave them a portion of his profits.

His reputation as a champion of the oppressed quickly spread. He attracted a sizable band of followers, even though they knew that, if they were captured, they would surely hang and their heads would be displayed on spikes atop the prison walls.

Early in his career Shane was arrested, clapped in irons, and sent under guard to Derry jail. When the

Shane probably used a pike like this to escape from the British soldiers. Then he "went on his keeping."

soldiers stopped along the way to eat, someone—perhaps Shane himself—proposed a jumping contest. Shane asked if he could compete, and the guards foolishly agreed. The moment they removed his shackles he made a dash for freedom.

The soldiers fired ineffectually, then gave chase. For ten miles Shane kept ahead of his pursuers, dodging bullets, scrambling over rocks, swimming across rivers. Finally, close to exhaustion, he found his way blocked by a deep gorge. The soldiers were closing in. He had only two choices: jump or be shot.

With weary legs he launched himself into the air and landed on a narrow ledge on the other side. Though he broke a leg, he managed to drag himself to a house whose owner set the broken bone. The spot where he jumped the gorge is still known as Shane's Leap.

There was no shortage of folk willing to provide aid and shelter, even though they risked being thrown in jail for it. Shane always made a point of repaying the debt. Once, a child whose family had helped the rapparees fell into the River Roe. When he came home, drenched but alive, he told his parents he had been rescued "by a big man with a beard who said his name was Shane."

The assistance of others who hated the English enabled Shane to elude the law for almost three decades —long enough to marry and raise two sons, who eventually joined him on his raids. The Derry Outlaw was finally betrayed by a local weaver who, legend has it, loved the woman who became Shane's wife. No doubt the man also resented paying protection money to his rival. In 1722, when Shane came to the weaver's cottage to collect the "tax," a group of soldiers were waiting.

This time he didn't bother to run. He was getting on in years, and the leg he'd broken years before pained him. He was taken to Derry jail. When his sons came to find him, they were seized too. An influential landowner secured a pardon for the outlaw but, since it didn't include his sons, Shane refused it. "I have only a few years left to live in any case," he said. "So, with God's blessing, I'll die with them."

When he stood on the scaffold with a rope around his neck and a son on either side, Shane spoke to those who had gathered. He thanked them for their support over the years and asked them to remember him in their prayers. Then he clasped his sons' hands in his and nodded to the hangman.

Six

The Butcher-Highwayman

Though the government kept on trying to discourage would-be highwaymen by publicly displaying the bodies of executed thieves, the strategy didn't prove very effective. A corpse in chains was a chilling sight, but it couldn't hope to counteract the constant stream of books, ballads, and legends that glamorized the high- wayman and his profession.

The brief career of Jack Sheppard and his daring escapes for prison spawned countless pamphlets and songs, several successful plays—and a number of imitators. A valet who cut the throat of his employer, Lord William Russell, confessed that he had been inspired by a popular drama about Sheppard that he had recently seen. In the wake of the crime, the Lord Chamberlain refused to license any play with the name "Jack Sheppard" in the title.

John Gay's 1720 musical play, *The Beggar's Opera*, created a scandal with its sympathetic portraits of under- world figures, including a gallant highwayman named Macheath. The play was meant to be a satire that poked fun at courtiers and politicians by comparing them to thieves. Nevertheless, moralists condemned it, and not

Captain Macheath, the hero of The Beggar's Opera, *was reputedly based on Jack Sheppard. Another character, Peachum, was probably modeled on Jonathan Wild, a notorious underworld figure who styled himself the "Thief-Taker General."*

without reason. When two teenage criminals were arrested, copies of *The Beggar's Opera* were discovered on them. Another seventeen-year-old thief admitted that he was "so delighted with the spirit and heroic character of Macheath, that on quitting the theatre he laid out his last guinea on the purchase of a pair of pistols, and stopped a gentleman on the highway."

No one knows how many youths were led astray by the deeds of William Nevison, the Yorkshire Rogue. But one Essex youth who grew up on the Nevison legend went on to earn a reputation that would far surpass his hero's. In fact, in time he would even be credited with Swift Nicks's most celebrated exploit, the ride to York.

Dick Turpin, who was born in the county of Essex in 1705, started his adult life in an ordinary enough fashion, as an apprentice butcher. At age twenty-one he married Rose Palmer, an innkeeper's daughter, and opened his own shop. Unfortunately he was not particular about where the meat he sold came from. When a local farmer traced two stolen sheep to Turpin's slaughterhouse, Dick abruptly retired from the trade and took up smuggling.

Then, apparently stirred by tales of gentlemanly rogues such as Nevison, he opted for the higher-class profession of highway robbery, choosing as his victims the very men who had recently been his partners. When the smugglers sought revenge, Turpin fled to Epping Forest, where he joined a brutal band of deer poachers and housebreakers known as Gregory's Gang.

Since the country still had no organized police force, the courts depended on informers to help bring highwaymen to justice. The rewards were substantial—up to forty pounds, plus the convicted man's horse and weapon, and any unclaimed valuables.

The reward system was widely abused. Professional "thief takers" regularly enticed young men to commit robberies —even providing them with a horse, a pistol, and detailed instructions— then handed the poor dupes over to the nearest constable and collected the reward.

Sometimes, though, the system got real results, especially when the reward was as large as the one hundred pounds offered for the members of Gregory's Gang. Early in 1735 someone squealed on them. As the thieves were carousing in a tavern,

According to tradition, Dick Turpin sometimes hid out in Epping Forest in a cave that is still known as Turpin's Cave.

the authorities arrived. Only two men got away; one was Dick Turpin, who jumped out of a window.

A few months later a newspaper reported that travelers were being accosted "by two highwaymen, supposed to be Turpin the Butcher and Rowden the

Pewterer, the remaining two of Gregory's Gang, who robbed them of their money and dismounted them." Apparently Turpin wasn't bothering to disguise himself. Later that month the two held up a Mr. Omar. Suspecting that the man recognized him, Turpin "would have shot him, but was prevented by the other, who pulled the pistol out of his hand."

This may have been unnecessary; Turpin wasn't much of a marksman. According to the *Country Journal,* when a victim's pistol misfired, Turpin cried, "Damn you, you have missed me, but I won't you." Nevertheless, his shot completely missed the mark. (Later, his poor aim was to have more serious consequences.)

In 1737 Turpin joined forces with another knight of the road, Tom King. Their partnership didn't last long. Turpin was foolish enough to steal a well-known race-horse named Whitestockings. The owner located the horse in a London stable, and lay in wait until Turpin and his partner turned up. Dick recognized the man and fired at him, but fatally wounded Tom King instead.

Turpin wasted no time in mourning his friend. Soon afterward a London newspaper reported that "Turpin, the renowned butcher-highwayman, committed a robbery almost every day this month." A royal proclamation offered a reward of two hundred pounds for his capture. It described him as "about thirty-five, five feet nine inches high, brown complexion, very much marked with smallpox."

Though *London Magazine* characterized him as a "mean and stupid wretch," Turpin was smart enough to

Most sources agree that Tom King met his end as a result of his friend's poor marksmanship, as portrayed here. But Turpin himself supposedly claimed that he only wounded his fellow outlaw and that King was later executed.

know when he wasn't welcome. He headed north to Nevison's home county of Yorkshire, where, under the alias of John Palmer, he posed as a respectable horse dealer. Despite some suspicious activity on Turpin's part, his new neighbors considered him "a good fellow" and "a good friend to everyone." Because of his obvious wealth, the gentlemen of the county accepted him as one of them. But it wasn't long before he revealed his true nature.

On the way home from a hunt, a companion teased Turpin about his shooting ability, claiming that he "couldn't hit a barn-yard fowl." Turpin proceeded to prove him wrong by plugging one of his landlord's game birds. When the landlord protested, Dick replied that if the man would wait until he reloaded, he would shoot him too. The threat led to an investigation, which revealed that "Mr. Palmer" was wanted in neighboring counties on charges of stealing sheep and horses.

Turpin was held in York Castle, in the very cell where Swift Nicks had awaited execution. He wrote a letter begging his brother in Essex to come and testify on his behalf at the trial. Unfortunately he neglected to pay the proper postage, and his brother, not recognizing the handwriting, returned the letter to the post office.

Curiously enough, the postmaster *did* recognize the script; he was formerly the local schoolmaster, who had taught Dick Turpin to read and write. Apparently he did not remember his old pupil fondly, for he hurried to York, where he identified Dick and collected the reward.

Turpin was sentenced to hang. Crowds of people came to gawk at the famous outlaw, who was "as jovial, merry, and frolicsome as if he had been perfectly at liberty and assured of a hundred years to come." When one visitor offered to bet anyone that the prisoner was not the celebrated Turpin, Dick whispered to the jailer, "Lay him the wager, and I'll go you halves!"

He kept up his air of unconcern all the way to the gallows—at least outwardly. As he mounted the ladder, one leg began to tremble. Impatiently, he stamped his

Dick Turpin's famous ride to York, a familiar subject of English plays, ballads, and folklore, was probably purely a novelist's invention.

foot to stop the shaking. He talked casually with the hangman as the noose went around his neck and then, without waiting to be forced, he leaped off the ladder. Whatever his other faults, Turpin was no coward.

His enduring reputation has little to do with his courage, though, or his success as a criminal. It's almost entirely the result of the romanticized stories that appeared after his death. He was already a legend by 1834, when William Harrison Ainsworth published *Rookwood,* the novel that would ensure the highwayman's immortality. The best-selling book tells the detailed and rousing story of an amazing (and very familiar-sounding) ride that Turpin supposedly made from London to York in a single day, setting such a fierce pace that his magnificent steed, Black Bess, perished from the effort.

Even today, folk in villages all along England's Great North Road point out relics and landmarks that featured in Turpin's famous ride. And at night some still report hearing the sound of Black Bess's ghostly hooves galloping by.

Seven

The Bow Street Runners and the Horse Patrol

By the time Dick Turpin went to the gallows in 1739, crime in and around London had become a problem too big to be ignored. Criminals were growing increasingly bold, threatening or attacking city officials, and even raiding prisons. Citizens clamored for safer streets and highways. But at the same time they disliked the notion of a permanent professional police force, fearing that it would be too costly and would pose a threat to individual freedom.

The keeping of the peace was entrusted to constables—ordinary men chosen by their peers to serve, without pay, for a year—and to the mostly ineffectual night watch, also known as the Charlies, after King Charles II. Novelist Henry Fielding described the Charlies as "poor, old, decrepit people . . . armed only with a pole, which some of them are scarce able to lift."

Fielding is best known today as the author of *Tom Jones*, but he contributed nearly as much to law enforcement as he did to literature. A former lawyer turned playwright, Fielding lost his income when the theater that produced his plays was closed down in 1748. He found a new position as a magistrate, or commissioner

When it came to apprehending criminals, Charlies, or city watchmen, were of little use. Horace Walpole witnessed a fleeing robber on horseback who, confronted by a Charlie, simply "rode over the watchman, almost killed him, and escaped."

of the peace, and immediately set about reforming things, firing constables who were incompetent or corrupt, then organizing and training those who were left.

In 1751 Fielding published an influential pamphlet, titled *An Enquiry into the Causes of the Late Increase of*

Gallant on the Gallows

The English highwayman was glorified not only for the dashing way he lived, but also for the grace and grit he displayed in the face of death. Henry Fielding wrote disapprovingly that "His Procession to *Tyburn*, and his last Moments there, are all triumphant; attended with the Compassion of the meek and tender-hearted, and with the Applause, Admiration, and Envy of all the bold and hardened."

The audience at the place of execution, which often numbered in the thousands, expected a pretty speech from the condemned man, and most of them obliged. Isaac Atkinson's last address was brief but bold. Smiling, he called to the crowd, "Gentlemen, there's nothing like a merry life and a short one!"

It was also traditional for the cart to stop at a tavern on the route, so the prisoner could have a last pint of ale—a custom begun by Philip Stafford, who downed a drink on his way to the gallows, then promised to pay for it on the way back.

Dick Hughes spent his final moments discussing with his wife the matter of who was obliged to pay for the rope. "The Sheriff, honey," said Dick. "Ah," replied his wife, "I wish I had known . . . for I have been and bought one already." "Well, well," said Dick, "perhaps it mayn't be lost; for it may serve a second husband."

Robbers, in which he attacked the audaciousness of highwaymen: "Have not some of these committed Robberies in open Day-light, in the Sight of many People, and have afterward rode solemnly and triumphantly through the neighbouring Towns without any Danger or Molestation[?]"

He also proposed practical measures for crime prevention that prompted the government to pass the Gin Act and the Act for Better Preventing Thefts and Robberies. The first controlled the sale of liquor, which

Not all condemned men were so calm or courageous. Paul Lewis acted brave and boastful enough in his cell at Newgate, but when the day of his execution arrived, he "lost all his assumed courage, his vauntings sank into trembling fears, and he became as abject as before he appeared hardened."

John Ashton's sanity gave way under the strain. He ran up the steps of the scaffold and began to dance about, shouting, "Look at me! I am Lord Wellington!" When the trapdoor was released, the rope proved so elastic that Ashton rebounded onto the platform, where he resumed cavorting and crying, "What do ye think of me? Am I not Lord Wellington now?" until the executioner pushed him off.

When authorities displayed an executed criminal in irons like these, the body usually didn't hang around for long. After dark, friends or family cut down the corpse—or the entire gibbet. If the body had been dipped in tar to preserve it, they might cremate it by setting it afire.

Fielding felt contributed to crime. The second made it a crime to receive and resell stolen property; "if there were no Receivers," wrote Fielding, "there would be no Thieves."

Fielding hired as an assistant his blind half brother, John. (John's handicap made him no less effective. He claimed to be able to recognize some three thousand criminals by their voices.) With the help of a small government grant, the two established England's first corps of professional detectives, the Bow Street Runners, and

Henry Fielding compared the streets and alleys of London to "a vast Wood or Forest, in which a Thief may harbour with as great Security, as Wild Beasts do in the Desarts [deserts] of Africa or Arabia."

began keeping a written record of all reported crimes and suspects. They quickly got results. According to a notice in the *General Advertiser,* "Near forty highwaymen, street robbers, burglars, rogues, vagabonds and cheats have been committed within a week by Justice Fielding."

The Runners' success was mainly confined to the city, though. A well-armed force of mounted police was needed to combat thieves on the highways. After Henry Fielding's death in 1754, John managed to get funding

At his office in Bow Street, Commissioner Fielding worked sixteen hours a day, training detectives and examining suspects, and still found time to create a new novel, Amelia, *published in 1751.*

for a horse patrol. In the first week of its existence only two robberies were committed on the main roads, and both perpetrators were caught.

The government, foolishly imagining that the problem was now under control, promptly cut off its funding. Just as promptly, the robberies resumed. No one was safe. The prime minister, the Prince of Wales, and the lord mayor were all victims of the latest crime spree. Finally, in 1805, the public outcry forced authorities to establish a new horse patrol, one made up mainly of experienced ex-cavalrymen.

The patrol was only one of several factors that conspired to make life difficult for robbers. The desolate stretches of heath that had been their favorite hunting grounds were gradually being fenced in and used for grazing. The condition of roads was improving; many were turned into turnpikes, with toll booths where police could easily intercept thieves. And the country's growing banking system allowed travelers to carry banknotes instead of gold or silver. The heyday of the English highwayman was fast coming to a close.

Eight

The Knight of the Natchez Trace

Though England was becoming civilized, the newly independent United States was still unsettled enough to offer plenty of opportunities for road inspectors. In fact, a number of frustrated English thieves concluded that a voyage to America would be a smart career move.

Not that there was any shortage of home-grown criminals. From their cavern hideout, the six Doane brothers terrorized New Jersey and Pennsylvania for nearly a decade before they were captured and hanged in 1788. Sam Mason, who once fought alongside Revolutionary War hero George Rogers Clark, made a postwar career of ambushing flatboats carrying cargo down the Mississippi River. The sadistic Harp brothers of Kentucky—known as Big Harp and Little Harp—specialized in murdering their victims in various brutal ways.

The earliest American outlaw who could really be considered a highwayman in the traditional mold was Joseph Thompson Hare, described in a popular biography as "the first great freebooter of the Republic."

Hare was born in Chester County, Pennsylvania, near the end of the eighteenth century and was raised in the slums of Philadelphia, Baltimore, and New York City.

As a young man, he apprenticed in the shop of a New York tailor, where he learned to appreciate fine clothing and fabrics—a trait that, years later, would prove to be his undoing.

After two years in the tailoring trade, Hare grew restless and joined the crew of a sailing ship. When they put in at the bustling port of New Orleans, Hare jumped ship. For a time he supported himself by picking pockets and looting homes, but he was always on the lookout for a more refined and profitable pursuit, and he soon found it.

Hare observed that traders from Kentucky and Tennessee regularly shipped merchandise down the Mississippi to Natchez or New Orleans, where they sold the goods at a substantial profit. Then, rather than fight their way upstream, they returned home via the trail known as the Natchez Trace, carrying large sums of money with them.

North of Natchez the trail led through a long, lonely stretch of swampy wilderness—an ideal place for a hold-up. Hare and three fellow thieves furnished themselves with horses and weapons, painted their faces with berry juice and stain made from tree bark, and surprised a party of travelers in a desolate spot. According to Hare's diary, "We took three hundred doubloons and five silver dollars, and four hundred French guineas, and 67 pieces the value of which I could not tell until I weighed them. I got twelve or thirteen thousand dollars all together."

A second robbery netted them seven thousand dollars. The gang set up a hideout "in a cleft rock, where

THE LIFE

OF THE

CELEBRATED MAIL ROBBER AND DARING HIGHWAYMAN,

JOSEPH THOMPSON HARE,

WHO COMMITTED DEPREDATIONS IN THE CITIES OF NEW YORK AND PHILADELPHIA TO THE AMOUNT OF NEARLY NINETY THOUSAND DOLLARS

ALSO, OF THE CRUEL AND FEROCIOUS PIRATE,

ALEXANDER TARDY.

PHILADELPHIA:

J. B. PERRY, No. 198 MARKET STREET.

NEW YORK:—NAFIS & CORNISH, 278 PEARL ST.

1847.

In the tradition of the "Newgate romances," which sensationalized the exploits of English highwaymen, this nineteenth-century pamphlet recounted the career of American bandit Joseph Hare.

Though troops began clearing and patrolling the Natchez Trace in 1801, travelers were in constant danger of being ambushed by bandits or by members of the Choctaw and Chickasaw tribes, who resented the intrusion of white settlers.

one rock jutted very much over another, and made a sort of cave." Despite the fact that they "had a good feather bed in our cave," it was not the sort of life a city boy like Hare was accustomed to. So much empty wilderness made him uneasy, especially when the wind blowing through the canebrake "made such a mournful rustling sound."

His nerves were frayed further when the robbery of a slave trader went awry. The trader pretended to hand over his pistol, but instead pulled the trigger; the shot blasted Hare's hat off his head. The highwayman decided it was time for some rest and relaxation in the big city. He and his companions headed for Nashville and then New Orleans, where they lived in luxury, dining and drinking and gambling until their money ran out. Then they returned to the Trace.

This time Hare endured the harsh, gloomy surroundings for only two months before escaping to the city again. Like the traditional English highwayman, he fancied himself a gentleman, so when one of his partners tried to force his attentions on an innocent Spanish girl, Hare came to her rescue. He gave his companion "as handsome a dressing as any man ever got. . . . I whipt him until he hollowed 'Enough!'" Thinking he had killed the man, Hare, along with his other two accomplices, fled to Pensacola, a military outpost in Spanish-held Florida.

Because Americans were growing increasingly determined to add Florida to the United States, relations with Spain were strained. Still, the amiable and outgoing Hare managed to make friends with a number of influential people—fortunately for him. As the three thieves were returning to American soil, they were arrested on suspicion of being spies, and thrown into prison. But Hare's new Florida friends showed up to testify on his behalf, and he and his men were set free.

Though the three took up their old trade again, relieving travelers on the Trace of some ten thousand dollars, Hare's conscience had begun to bother him. Between holdups he argued with his companions about the morality of what they were doing, and even "read them from John Wesley's magazine," a religious tract. It wasn't long before the gang split up; no doubt the others were tired of Hare's preaching.

Despite his qualms, Hare couldn't stop himself from holding up one more victim. He wrote that, after the robbery, "As I was riding along very rapidly to get out of the reach of pursuit, I saw standing right across the road, a beautiful white horse, as white as snow. . . . When I approached him . . . he disappeared in an instant, which made me very uneasy. . . . I think this white horse was Christ, and that he came to warn me of my sins, and to make me fear and repent."

Shaken, Hare stopped for the night at a house— a serious miscalculation. A posse raised by his victim tracked him down there and seized him. He spent the next five years in jail, reading the Bible and writing in his diary. One entry reads, "Let not anyone be induced to turn highwayman by reading this book and seeing the great sums of money I have robbed, for it is a desperate life, full of danger, and sooner or later ends at the gallows."

Anyone who saw Hare's remorseful manner would naturally expect that, upon his release in 1817, he would choose the straight and narrow path. Instead he chose the highway to Baltimore, where he held up a mail coach carrying a bank shipment of more than sixteen thousand dollars—the largest prize ever won by a knight of the road up to that time. To discourage pursuit, he tied one of the passengers to a wheel of the coach. The man begged Hare to return his watch, a family heirloom. As the highwayman raised the lantern to look for the watch, the light clearly revealed his features.

Two days later, while Hare was in a Baltimore tailor's shop, spending some of his profits on the fine clothing he was so fond of, the passenger from the coach happened to walk in. Recognizing Hare at once, he turned him over to the police.

For much of his life Joseph Thompson Hare had tried to carry on the tradition of the gallant, devil-may-care highwayman. But when he was led to the gallows in September 1818, he broke with tradition. He made no brave speeches from the scaffold, and drank no farewell toast. His last moments on earth were spent reading his Bible and praying.

GLOSSARY

Ainsworth, William Harrison (1805–1882) English author of thirty-nine mostly forgotten novels, including one entitled *Jack Sheppard.*

canebrake A thicket of cane, a tall, bamboolike grass native to the southern United States.

chapbook A small book or pamphlet containing popular tales, ballads, and nursery rhymes. Chapbooks were sold on the street by merchants known as chapmen.

Charles I (1600–1649) King of England from 1625 until his execution by the English Parliament.

Charles II (1630–1685) Oldest son of Charles I. Exiled to Holland and France after his father's death, he was restored to the throne in 1660.

Cromwell, Oliver (1599–1658) A politician and soldier who fought against Charles I and Charles II in the English Civil War. Though Parliament offered to make him king, Cromwell settled for the title of Lord Protector, which he held from 1653 until his death. After Charles II regained power, he had Cromwell's body dug up, hanged, and beheaded.

Defoe, Daniel (1660–1731) English author famous for his novels *Robinson Crusoe* and *Moll Flanders.* Defoe had a continuing fascination with criminals.

De Quincey, Thomas (1785–1859) English essayist best known for his autobiographical work, *Confessions of an Opium Eater.*

dropsy A disorder also known as edema, in which excessive fluid builds up in the body's tissues. The condition is often a result of heart or kidney disease.

Fielding, Henry (1707–1754) English dramatist, essayist, and novelist. His comic novel *Tom Jones* was made into a popular film in 1963.

Flanders A former French province that included parts of what are now France, Belgium, and the Netherlands.

flintlock   A type of musket or pistol introduced in the late 1500s. Its spring-loaded hammer holds a piece of flint. When the flint is struck against a metal plate, it produces a spark, igniting a charge of gunpowder.

gallows   A wooden frame from which condemned criminals were hanged. The gallows at Tyburn consisted of three uprights supporting three cross beams that formed a triangle large enough to hang several criminals at once.

Gay, John (1685–1732)   English poet and playwright. His phenomenally successful *The Beggar's Opera* inspired the musical play *The Threepenny Opera*, which features the popular song "Mack the Knife."

gibbet   A frame similar to a gallows but with a projecting arm that was generally used to display the corpse of an executed criminal.

matchlock   An early style of musket whose firing mechanism consisted of a lighted "match," or slow-burning fuse, that was used to set off the gunpowder.

Natchez Trace   A road that traversed five hundred miles of wilderness between Natchez, Mississippi, and Nashville, Tennessee. The United States Army began clearing the route in 1801, following an old Indian trail.

Newgate   A dark, damp London prison that housed short-term convicts, including those awaiting execution. Rather than being supported by government funds, Newgate was a private enterprise, and prisoners were obliged to pay for its "services."

Noyes, Alfred (1880–1958)   English poet, critic, and novelist.

Tyburn   An area of London where two streams, the Tye and the Bourne, once converged. It was the site of public executions from 1571 until 1783.

Walpole, Horace (1717–1797)   Author, prolific letter writer, and son of English prime minister Sir Robert Walpole. His book *The Castle of Otranto* is considered the first Gothic romance, a type of novel characterized by spooky settings and mysterious, sometimes supernatural incidents.

TO LEARN MORE ABOUT HIGHWAYMEN

Books—*Nonfiction*

Ross, Stewart. *Bandits & Outlaws.* Fact or Fiction Series. Brookfield, CT: Copper Beech, 1995.

  This volume in the Fact or Fiction Series tells the story of real and legendary bandits, from Spartacus to Robin Hood to modern-day badguys, with the emphasis on dispelling their romantic image. Several pages are devoted to famous highwaymen. Heavily illustrated with drawings and photos.

Books—*Fiction*

Fleischman, Sid. *The Whipping Boy.* New York: Greenwillow, 1986.

  In this Newbery Award-winning novel, a prince and his servant become involved with highwaymen, and discover what it's like to be in each other's shoes.

Noyes, Alfred. *The Highwayman.* New York: Lothrop, 1983.

  Charles Mikolaycak's dark, dramatic illustrations make Noyes's story-poem even more romantic.

On-line Information*

http://www.law.utexas.edu/lpop/etext

  The complete text of the five-volume *Newgate Calendar,* which offers contemporary accounts of various seventeenth- and eighteenth-century criminals, including Mary Frith, Claude Duval, William Nevison, Dick Turpin, and William Davis.

http://www.dilley.demon.co.uk/royston/ppl/turpin.htm

  This website about the village of Hempstead, England, Dick Turpin's birthplace, includes stories about its most notorious native son.

* *Websites change from time to time. For additional on-line information, check with the media specialist at your local library.*

Historic Sites

Natchez Trace Parkway Visitor Center, 2680 Natchez Trace Parkway, Tupelo, MS 38801.

Offers films, books, and other information about the history of the Natchez Trace. Telephone: 1-800-305-7417.
Website: http://www.nps.gov/natr

BIBLIOGRAPHY

Billett, Michael. *Highwaymen and Outlaws*. London: Arms and Armour, 1997.

Coates, Robert M. *The Outlaw Years: The History of the Land Pirates of the Natchez Trace*. New York: Literary Guild, 1930.

Daggett, David. *The Life and Adventures of Joseph Mountain, A Negro Highwayman*. Bennington, VT: Haswell, 1791.

Elman, Robert. *Badmen of the West*. London: Ridge Press, 1974.

Fairfax-Blakeborough, J., ed. *Legends of Highwaymen and Others*. Detroit: Singing Tree Press, 1971.

Fielding, Henry. *An Enquiry Into the Causes of the Late Increase of Robbers, & c.* New York: AMS Press, 1975.

Gay, John. *The Beggar's Opera*. New York: Harper & Row, 1973.

Gollomb, Joseph. *Master Highwaymen*. New York: Macaulay, 1927.

Hibbert, Christopher. *Highwaymen*. New York: Delacorte, 1967.

Macaulay, Thomas Babington. *Macaulay's History of England: From the Accession of James II*. London: Dent, 1966.

McCallen, Jim. *'Stand and Deliver!'—Stories of Irish Highwaymen*. Dublin: Mercier Press, 1993.

Prassel, Frank Richard. *The Great American Outlaw: A Legacy of Fact and Fiction*. Norman, OK: University of Oklahoma, 1993.

Pringle, Patrick. *Stand and Deliver*. New York: Dorset, 1991.

Untermeyer, Louis, ed. *The Golden Treasury of Poetry*. New York: Golden Press, 1959.

NOTES ON QUOTES

The quotations in this book are from the following sources:

Introduction
Page 6, "He'd a French cocked-hat": Untermeyer, ed., *The Golden Treasury of Poetry*, p. 131.
Page 7, "was a rebel": Hibbert, *Highwaymen*, p. 119.
"in general, of a superior class": *Highwaymen*, p. 13.
Page 8, "the whole affair": *Highwaymen*, p. 26.
Page 9, "queer law" and "is robbed": *Highwaymen*, p. 64.

Chapter One: The Roaring Girl
Page 10, "strength, health, agility": Pringle, *Stand and Deliver*, p. 269.
"lusty and sturdy": *Stand and Deliver*, p. 55.
"a voice that will drown": *Stand and Deliver*, p. 56.
"A very tomrig": *Stand and Deliver*, p. 55.
Page 12, "wept bitterly" and "she was maudlin": *Stand and Deliver*, p. 57.

Chapter Two: The French Footman
Page 15, "generally very polite": *Highwaymen*, p. 15.
"would sooner part" and "Since you value": *Highwaymen*, p. 16.
Page 16, "unblameably, unless": *Stand and Deliver*, p. 101.
Page 17, "maids, widows and wives": *Highwaymen*, p. 38.
Page 18, "great fondness": *Stand and Deliver*, p. 99.
Page 19, "All the villians": *Stand and Deliver*, p. 26.
Page 20, "Sir, your lady": *Stand and Deliver*, p. 102.
"you have forgot" and "civilly takes": *Stand and Deliver*, p. 103.
"crowds of ladies": *Highwaymen*, p. 40.
Page 22, "Here lies Du Vall": *Stand and Deliver*, p. 105.

Chapter Three: The Yorkshire Rogue
Page 23, "a noted place": *Stand and Deliver*, p. 137.
Page 24, "real name was": Fairfax-Blakeborough, ed., *Legends of Highwaymen and Others*, p. 213.
Page 25, "lusty, well-looking" and "the ringleader": *Stand and Deliver*, p. 124.
"tall in stature": *Stand and Deliver*, p. 134.

Page 26, "let them passe": *Stand and Deliver*, p. 130.
"holding on the North" and "what o'clock": *Stand and Deliver*, p. 138.
"it was impossible" and "on assurance": *Stand and Deliver*, p. 138.
Page 27, "Upon this the King": *Stand and Deliver*, p. 139.
Page 28, "the principal business": Daggett, *The Life and Adventures of Joseph Mountain, A Negro Highwayman*, p. 4.
"resolved to quit": *The Life and Adventures of Joseph Mountain*, p. 10.
"though singularly vicious": *The Life and Adventures of Joseph Mountain*, p. 11.
"miss Nancy Allingame" and "exhausted all the property": *The Life and Adventures of Joseph Mountain*, p. 20.
"robbed in most": *The Life and Adventures of Joseph Mountain*, p. 25.
"a respectable young girl": *The Life and Adventures of Joseph Mountain*, p. 1.
"There can be no": *The Life and Adventures of Joseph Mountain*, p. 26.
"in a country": *The Life and Adventures of Joseph Mountain*, p. 27.
Page 31, "The Bird is": *Legends of Highwaymen and Others*, p. 224.
"I've not robb'd": *Legends of Highwaymen and Others*, pp. 218–219.

Chapter Four: The Golden Farmer
Page 34, "I don't care": *Stand and Deliver*, p. 114.
Page 35, "What, have you" and "I have no more": *Stand and Deliver*, p. 110.
"he can't be hanged": *Highwaymen*, p. 57.

Chapter Five: The Derry Outlaw
Page 39, "by a big man": McCallen, *'Stand and Deliver!'—Stories of Irish Highwaymen*, p. 21.
Page 40, "I have only": *'Stand and Deliver!'—Stories of Irish Highwaymen*, p. 23.

Chapter Six: The Butcher-Highwayman
Page 43, "so delighted with": *Highwaymen*, pp. 104, 113.
Page 44, "by two highwaymen" : *Stand and Deliver*, p. 211.
Page 45, "would have shot": *Stand and Deliver*, p. 211.
"Damn you": *Stand and Deliver*, p. 213.
"Turpin, the renowned": *Stand and Deliver*, p. 215.
"mean and stupid": *Stand and Deliver*, p. 218.
Page 46, "a good fellow" and "a good friend": *Legends of Highwaymen and Others*, p. 245.

Page 47, "couldn't hit": *Legends of Highwaymen and Others*, p. 244.
"as jovial, merry" and "Lay him the wager": *Stand and Deliver*, p. 218.

Chapter Seven: The Bow Street Runners and the Horse Patrol
Page 50, "poor, old decrepit": *Stand and Deliver*, p. 233.
Page 52, "His Procession to *Tyburn*": *An Enquiry Into the Causes*, p. 121.
"Gentlemen, there's nothing": *Stand and Deliver*, p. 32.
"The Sheriff, honey": *Stand and Deliver*, pp. 186–187.
"Have not some": Fielding, *An Enquiry Into the Causes of the Late Increase of Robbers, & c.*, p. 94.
Page 53, "lost all his assumed" and "Look at me!": *Highwaymen*, p. 91.
"What do ye think": *Highwaymen*, p. 92.
"if there were": *An Enquiry Into the Causes*, p. 68.
Page 54, "Near forty highwaymen": *Highwaymen*, p. 77.

Chapter Eight: The Knight of the Natchez Trace
Page 57, "the first great freebooter": Elman, *Badmen of the West*, p. 36.
Page 58, "We took three hundred": Coates, *The Outlaw Years: The History of the Land Pirates of the Natchez Trace*, p. 89.
"in a cleft rock": *The Outlaw Years*, p. 90.
Page 60, "had a good": *The Outlaw Years*, p. 90.
"made such a mournful": *The Outlaw Years*, p. 91.
Page 61, "as handsome a dressing": *The Outlaw Years*, pp. 99–100.
Page 62, "read them from": *The Outlaw Years*, p. 102.
Page 62, "As I was riding": *The Outlaw Years*, pp. 102–103.
"Let not anyone": *The Outlaw Years*, p. 97.

INDEX

Page numbers for illustrations are in boldface